UNSHAKABLE

31 Devotionals To Keep You Steady And Sure Through The Shaking

Dr. Debbie Lanier

DEDICATION

As I complete my third book, I recognize a distinct thread interlacing them all like a triple-braided cord: my generations...behind me, before me, and alongside me.

My first book honored my Mama's overcoming life. Her passionate journey of faith through every kind of hard thing became my first seminary. She lit the fire in me!

My second book honored my grandchildren not yet born. I pray for them now like they are already here! They will stand on our shoulders of great faith! THEY WILL!

I devote this book to the one who has remained completely devoted to me since the first day we met. Paul Francis Lanier, III...he's my one true love! He does a thousand things well and hears from God in greater dimensions than anybody I know. So, it shouldn't surprise anyone that he discerned God's Calling upon my living long before I did.

Forty years ago, these two unlikely lovers hitched themselves as one. I knew I loved him, but marrying a minister thrust me into a role I did not desire AT ALL!

Thoughts of it scared the bejeezus out of me! Of all the things a little girl dreams, THIS was NEVER on my radar.

My hesitation about ministry proved so severe that my husband proposed three different times! I eventually realized, while I could live without ministry's mantle, I could never live without him!

We lay in bed, late at night, exploring the Gospels together throughout that first year of marriage. Devouring God's Word so intimately in that season fueled my desire to know Jesus all the more.

I began as a Pastor's wife, but it didn't last long. God's call (and my husband's nudge!) shoved me straight to the front lines of full-time ministry.

I enlisted in seminary to wrangle my way through bootcamp. There was only one cotton-pickin' female in most of those classes. (That would be me!) Feelings of inadequacy made me want to cry AND crawl beneath the table. These seasoned male ministers could surely run laps around this young chick. There my scrawny self sat, braced for the worst! But I'll have you know, by the end of my first class, I realized something extraordinary.

Sitting under my husband's preaching all those years gave me the unfair advantage. I knew more about theology and ministry than that vast number of men who had led flocks for decades!

I don't say this to brag. I say it because I rose to the top of my classes largely because of my favorite guy's preaching. I relished years of his "crash courses" long before enrolling in seminary. To this day, Paul Francis Lanier, III is my all-time favorite preacher! He won't allow himself to coast in God because there's always more awaiting us.

He helped me find ME! Ministry is no longer what I do; it's who I am. If I stopped today, I would shrivel up and die! I can't live even one day without God actively at work in my story. His Word is like fire shut up in my bones, FOR REAL Y'ALL!

Just as my doting husband helped me find my truest self, I pray that within these pages you will find your truest self too! From this place, your life finds its purpose! Friend, you were made for SO MUCH MORE!

Say this out loud with me:
I AM who God says I am!
I HAVE what God says I have!
I CAN DO what He says I can do!
I Surely Can! I Surely WILL!

Contents

PREFACE

"Unshakable." Is any word more incongruent with this moment in history? As I type these thoughts, every entity, every platform, literally shakes from its foundations!

In recent days, images from the Middle East, so barbaric that our mind shuts off to protect itself, churn from social media. Chatter of World War III reverberates across the airwaves at fever pitch as terrorists behead infants, burn children alive, and rape women like savages...all with glee in their eyes. It's unconscionable!

Such horrors once felt far away. But with the collapse of institutions and the demolition of our cities, safety and sanity have all but disappeared. Devastation breathes and breeds among us.

The world has been through a thing in recent years. Casualties prove incalculable! We can count the loved ones who died. But statistics do not capture the untold others we cherish who just stopped living. Fear found a home in them. It forever changed their constitution from the inside out.

And just when we survivors feel like we're getting back to our feet, a gnawing knot in the pit of our stomach knows what we don't want to know. More pandemonium is coming!

We're not merely coming out of a thing. We're bracing for upheaval that makes previous perplexities resemble child's play.

I don't say this to frighten you. I say it to prepare you! In fact, this whole book is about readying you. If you're not equipped for the coming, you'll be stacked with the next round of casualties. BUT THAT'S NOT YOUR STORY!

"A wise person discerns the danger ahead and prepares himself, but the naïve simpleton never looks ahead and suffers the consequences." (Proverbs 27:12 tPt)

We discern the times and prepare ourselves like we've already read the last chapter! We know Who triumphs, and we position ourselves on the winning side!

Though we loathe the predictability of unpredictability in this hour, God warned us that deception would shake the earth. In fact, He said "all of creation will be shaken so that only UNSHAKABLE things will remain." (Hebrews 12:27 NLT)

What are the UNSHAKABLE things that will remain?

Jesus said, *"The earth and sky will wear out and fade away before one Word I speak loses its power or fails to accomplish its purpose!"* (Matthew 24:35 tPt) In other words, He assures us it's impossible for HIS WORD to cave when everything around us collapses.

Listen friend, when we choose every new day to build our lives upon the Unshakable Word of God that has withstood every test in all of time and space, we can remain immovable as we walk amid the rubble heaps of our time!

I carry a boldness these days that doesn't make sense to those wobbling with worry and frozen in fear. I wish you could look into my eyes to discern its authenticity!

I desperately want you to possess this UNSHAKABLE certainty too!

Stop taking your cues from the living dead! Refuse to follow those walking in quicksand! It's time to STAND on God's Immovable Infrastructure that never trembles!

We're either going to dwell or die. Dwell in the Unconquerable Word or die…these are our options! Doom belongs to those in darkness. Victory is OUR portion! Y'all, this fight is fixed!

Of all moments to be alive, God made YOU for now! Not Moses or Elijah, not Peter or the Apostle Paul. He created YOU as a force to be reckoned with in these last moments of human history! He trusts YOU to be His solution in the earth! I DO TOO!

Let's dive into HIS UNSHAKABLE WORD together so that we walk through these uncertain times unafraid, undeterred, unrelenting…UNSHAKABLE!

Jeremiah 17:7-8 (VOICE & MSG)

"Blessed are the ones who trusts in ME ALONE!
I will be their confidence.
They're like trees replanted in Eden,
putting down roots near the rivers—
Never a worry through the hottest of summers,
never dropping a leaf,
Serene and calm through droughts,
bearing fresh fruit every season,
no matter what it faces."

1

RECALCULATING

Ephesians 3:18-19 (MSG)
*"I ask Him that with both feet planted firmly on love,
you'll be able to take in with all followers of Jesus
the extravagant dimensions of Christ's love.
Reach out and experience the breadth!
Test its length! Plumb the depths! Rise to the heights!
Live full lives, full in the fullness of God."*

Which "maps app" gets you where you're going? Don't you hate that nagging voice that practically sneers, *"Recalculating"*? Perhaps you veered only slightly from your destination. It still pauses you to get back on track!

SO…let's put first things first. As we dive into these transforming days together, let's identify where we are and do some recalculating of our own before we charge forward!

You Can't Get To Where You're Going If You Don't Recognize Where You Are!

God desires to clear the clutter clinging to your heart so you can catapult yourself fully into these pages ready to receive God's extravagant deposits. Lean in. Listen with your whole heart. God is speaking to you (yes, YOU!)!

You didn't mean to, but on some level, you checked out...or at the very least, you stepped back. Your heart, once laid so tender before the Lord, now seeks to conceal its callouses.

Of course, you love Him. But your life seems stuck at a standstill despite your prayers. Though you believe God for others' needs, you ever so gradually stopped trusting at the gut level for your own.

Your love toward Jesus no longer oozes with passion. It flickers with hopes that you can somehow regain that zealous love you felt when you first entrusted Him with your all.

Worse, you carry this gnawing suspicion that God carries frustration with you, too. (You know it's true!)

All this has a way of shutting down your heart, which is EXACTLY what the enemy of your soul wants!

Listen friend, Jesus is infinitely *kinder than kind.* His delight over you extends far beyond your heart's capacity to believe. Look at today's verse that describes the EXTRAVAGANT DIMENSIONS of Jesus's unconditional love toward YOU! His deep affection for YOU has not waivered even a smidgen!

Just because you conceded to unbelief doesn't mean He did! Just because your love for Him falters at times doesn't mean His does!

Get still in this reality right now. Linger. Lean into His bosom. Stay here until you sense Jesus's embrace wrapped around your wilted soul.

YOU are Jesus' bride, His prized possession! YOU!

Your bridegroom did the unthinkable because His love for YOU could do no less! Despite your fickle fluctuations, this Lover willingly endured torture, even excruciating death, to call you...HIS! (You've heard this so often that you just missed it. Read it again! Absorb this outrageous devotion toward YOU!)

Friend, God is not distant, unaware, or insensitive to your needs. He is closer than the mention of His Name!

I urge you…sit before Him. Feast on His Word in these pages. Cry to Him from the deep places. This doting Lover will resurrect those hungers you once felt toward Him. He'll prove all over again that He has not changed His affections toward you.

If you'll let God do the recalculating, He'll lead you back to that hope that seems buried. He'll ignite new passions for Him that supersede any delight you've known. He'll not only restore you; He'll take you to higher heights and deeper depths.

I'm praying in these days together that you feel the flicker erupt into untamable flames! I'm believing by God that your heart will open wide and your child-like trust in Him will intensify as you experience His delight for YOU!

As this devoted Lover bends low to get where you are and scoops you up with affection that has no conditions, may you become "filled FULL in the fullness of God!"

What Difference Will This WORD Make In Me?

We have exposed a thing so we can address a thing. From this place, we cast off shame and condemnation. We abide in the extravagant dimensions of Jesus' love!

Read today's verse in several translations. Meditate on this Word for YOU throughout this day! His affections for YOU stay steady and sure!

2

A HUMBLING INVITATION

1 Corinthians 3:9 (tPt)
"WE ARE COWORKERS WITH GOD
and you are God's cultivated garden,
the house He is building."

Laugh if you want, but I STILL bake Christmas cookies with my grown children. We've laughed and loved through this tradition since before they were old enough to remember the memory!

My heart smiles to remember those little flour-smudged faces and sprinkle-filled floors. Oh, the mess! But oh, the delight! The sweetness of those moments surpassed the sweetness of the cookies (and still does).

Any sane person watching this exhilarating catastrophe might surely wonder why I didn't just bake the cookies myself. After all, I could have accomplished twice as much in half the time without needing disaster-relief afterward.

Sure, if the goal was strictly to create cookies, it would have made perfect sense to zip proficiently through it myself. But sheer delight transpired from deepening bonds with my children as we teamed together. Those moments brought combustible joy to my heart (and still do)!

Does it sound blasphemous to consider that God desires to partner with us, too?

We're talking about the Creator of every good thing in our life, the One who formed us in our mama's womb! THAT God!

The One who possesses ALL Power and ALL Knowledge...this Good Father is in need of NOTHING! He's utterly self-sufficient! He's the God who was here long before there was anybody here to tell Him He was God!

This Magnificent King actually *chooses to partner with US!*

While He could do anything effortlessly Himself, God so delights to be with US that He'd rather clean up the mess we make than do it without us! WOW! How humbling yet empowering too!

This All-Knowing Father is fully aware of our frailties. He knows we spill milk, drop dishes, and break things into a thousand tiny pieces. (You know it's true!)

We carry this proclivity to try things all by ourselves until we're clobbered by our own arrogance.

There Are Some Things We CAN'T Do Without God. And There Are Some Things God WON'T Do Without Us!

This Loving Father extends Promises to us throughout each page of Scripture. But friends, these promises are not guarantees; they are invitations.

God invites us to partner with Him to establish that promise in our living and into our world! He could do it entirely on His own with His hands tied behind His back. Yet God welcomes us to labor WITH Him, not merely FOR Him.

C.S. Lewis wrote, "For He [God] seems to do nothing of Himself which He can possibly delegate to His creatures. He commands us to do slowly and blunderingly what He could do perfectly and in the twinkling of an eye." (*The World's Last Night and Other Essays, p.8-9*)

But why? He simply likes it better when we do it with Him. It's that simple!

This Loving Lord rushes to pick up even the pieces we've shattered beyond recognition, so we can get back to doing that thing with Him! What a Father!

Friend, I don't know what promise from God you're waiting to see fulfilled. But the Lord sent me today to nudge you into action. He's waiting on US to get in the kitchen with Him! Let's roll up those sleeves and get to baking!

What Difference Will This WORD Make In Me?
What action can you take today to partner WITH God? He doesn't want you to do it FOR Him. Neither does He want to merely do it FOR you. God wants to do it WITH you! ACT in a way that accomplishes God's Will in the earth, then watch Him give you all you need to do it well!

3

RAISE YOUR SHIELD!

Ephesians 6:16 (CEV)
*"Let your faith be like a shield, and you will
be able to stop all the flaming arrows
of the evil one."*

Did you know that as you wipe sleep from your eyes each new morning, you stand upright and shuffle smack-dab into a warzone? You can't see the weapons targeting you, but it only takes a few short minutes to feel their force.

Here's the long and the short of it—a battle rages in the spirit realm for your soul. satan seeks to steal, kill, and destroy you! (John 10:10) These aren't my words; they came out of Jesus' mouth! This will make you want to run for the hills until you realize that Jesus offers you abundant LIFE…meaning, you have everything you need to completely devastate the adversary seeking to devastate you!

As the Apostle Paul penned today's verse, he envisioned the Roman soldiers guarding him in prison. Who goes into battle without a shield? Laying it down, even for minute, completely exposes you to the enemy's cheap shots.

A soldier's shield proved to be more than a showpiece. It covered the whole body. What's more, six layers of leather clad its iron frame. This armor endured the fiercest fights. No matter how long or how hard the enemy attacked, nothing penetrated it.

Get this—to prevent the leather from becoming stiff, each morning before the soldier ate his Wheaties *(I just lost the young readers!)*, he reached for a vial of oil. He rubbed that oil meticulously into the shield to keep it pliable and battle-ready. Skipping this daily practice meant defeat or death. True soldiers would never dream of overlooking the oil!

One more thing. Just before stepping onto the battlefield, warriors often soaked their shields in water. The saturated shields extinguished the fiery darts launched at them. In other words, the enemy's attacks proved harmless to those prepared for the confrontation.

Friends, are you getting this? We are at war! There's no getting around it. But in God, you've got everything you need to win! He has given you Himself as a *wrap-around* shield! (Psalms 7:10) Ever-growing Faith in Jesus protects us. I'm not talking about Faith borrowed from our parents or Faith that quotes Scripture every now and then. I'm talking about the kind of Faith that gets a fresh coat of anointing each new day! I'm talking about the kind of Faith that soaks so consumingly in God's Word that we wholeheartedly believe He means EVERYTHING He said!

When We Forget To Nourish Our Faith For Even A Day, We Leave Ourselves Completely Exposed! From That Vulnerable Position, The Enemy of Our Soul Has His Way With Us.

We must stop giving him the upper hand. RAISE YOUR SHIELD!!!

Faith in God's Word arms you to the teeth! You roll right through the attacks like an army tank, moving through the mayhem without flinching.

So, wipe the sleep from your eyes, stop shuffling, and reach for the oil! We've got this because we've got HIM!

What Difference Will This WORD Make In Me?

Put God's Word in YOUR mouth. Say it out loud. Do it again. Now write it down. Keep it before you continuously this day. Every time you speak it, it gets deeper in you, helping you to believe it all the more. His Word in your mouth gives you the confidence to RAISE YOUR SHIELD and Win!

4

TO SEE WITHOUT SEEING

John 1:29 (NKJV)
*"The next day John saw Jesus coming toward him
and said, "Behold, the Lamb of God
who takes away the sins of the world!"*

John the Baptist...wasn't he an odd guy? He didn't fit in anywhere. He dressed weird and talked strange. (We won't even get into his eccentric eating habits.)

It's safe to say that John was rough around the edges. Every word from his mouth sliced the air. This prophet's every proclamation provoked political powers and riled religionists right into a tailspin.

So, one would expect more of the same when this burly type saw Jesus approaching him that day at the

Jordan River. Yet, the encounter proved nothing of the sort. As the prophet witnessed this Jesus from Nazareth approaching, John's countenance cued the crowd that something completely "other" was happening in their midst.

In that moment, this fierce fella stopped yelling Truth and stood in absolute awe. His stammering lips uttered, with a completely convinced heart, "Behold, the Lamb of God who takes away the sins of the world."

Of course, today we don't use verbiage like, "Behold! Somebody important is coming!" But most of us know the absolute awe of a moment we discern to be emphatically more significant than we are.

"Behold" doesn't just mean to casually glance. It means to "Let Him impress Himself upon you!" It means to gaze so attentively that you become overwhelmed with Him and all He is making available to you!

That's what this firebrand, John, felt that day...absolute awe! This rugged rebel stood utterly overwhelmed by the significance of the One who stepped onto the scene offering hope we couldn't attain any other way. Jesus came to alter the trajectory of our messed-up story forever.

John only knew in part the fullest revelation of who Jesus was, yet even that part caused him to stop everything and stand reverently in jaw-dropping astonishment and adoration.

Listen Friend,
To See Or "Behold" Everything In Life
Except The Lamb Of God...
Well, That Means You Have Seen
Everything In Life
EXCEPT THE ONE THING
Worth Beholding!

To "behold" the best this world has to offer without seeing the Lamb of God—the One that stood in your place and became sin so you didn't have to live in it— that is no life at all! It's merely death in slow motion.

To miss "beholding" Jesus, to miss the opportunity for the Messiah to impress Himself into the innermost crevices of you, is to miss out on everything you were created to crave and consume. In fact, it's missing out entirely!

To behold everything but Jesus is like seeing a light from the outside of a beautiful spacious home that you've always dreamed of living in. You see it from a distance but you are completely separated from all that makes that place home. You cannot feel the warmth inside or the rest and refuge that was built with YOU in mind. It's like you see without seeing!

I don't know what you are beholding this day, but I know who is beholding you! Jesus longs to press Himself deeply into the marrow of your bones. He desires to bring every dead thing and dormant dream back to life in you! Jesus yearns to supercharge your entire story in such a way that every chapter reads like the greatest adventure of your life!

I can say with absolute certainty that I want NOTHING in this life impressed into me more than Jesus! If I miss Him, I miss it all! DON'T MISS HIM!

What Difference Will This WORD Make In Me?
Step back from the familiarity of what you know about Jesus. As you speak His Name, the LORD draws near to you this very day. As He draws near, BEHOLD Him! Let the gift of Jesus Himself and all He offers you overwhelm you this day!

5

WHOSE ADVERSARY?

Luke 10:18-19 (tPt)
*"Jesus replied, "I watched satan topple until he fell
suddenly from Heaven like lightning to the ground.
Now you understand that I have imparted to you
ALL My authority to trample over his kingdom.
You will trample upon every demon before you and
overcome every power satan possesses.
Absolutely nothing will be able to harm you
as you walk in this authority!"*

With the battle between good and evil increasingly
obvious, we tend to assume it must be this epic
confrontation between God and satan. We tell
ourselves we know how it's all going to end, but it sure
seems like an all-out brawl! And let's be honest, in

these times in which we live...it often feels like hell is prevailing.

Friend, *nothing could be further from the Truth!* Jesus has no adversary! NONE!!!!

You know this, right?!!!

The name "satan" means "adversary," but he is OUR adversary, not God's. Jesus mentions that moment when satan wanted to be worshipped rather than worship the One who made him. Jesus said, "I watched satan fall like lightning!" In other words, satan fell hard and fast! *Kaput!* Jesus watched, then carried on like it was nothing! THERE WAS ABSOLUTELY NO CONTEST! And there is STILL no contest between them!

Our God Has No Equal!
He Has No Rival!
There Is No Competitor!
NONE!

The battle rages within OUR soul! Our enemy incessantly seeks to deter, distract, and derail us from living in the blessing God intended for us. This adversary ultimately pursues our annihilation! That's no exaggeration!

Hell ruthlessly and relentlessly strategizes our destruction, while we too often remain casually careless in seeking our God who gives us the authority and power to destroy the enemy's plots against us.

satan challenges our authority because *he has none*! He surely carries an agenda that tries to convince us he has the upper hand. It's all a ploy…unless we play his game!

As we press into the Lord who loves us and gave His very best for us, as we lay our whole lives on His altar and receive all He has with our name on it, hell has no authority over us. But we surely carry authority and power over him!

Jesus holds the keys to ultimate victory! He conquered hell and the grave. If we are in Christ and He is active in us, that means we carry those same keys!

Hell may try to leverage situations to steal our peace, but friend, it's only scare tactics! The enemy of our soul holds no power over us, our purpose, or our destiny unless we relinquish it to him…AND WE WON'T!

Walk steady and sure today! We've steeped our lives in the One who has no adversary. This God gives us everything we need to sit the devil down and watch us live as MORE THAN CONQUERORS THROUGH CHRIST JESUS!

What Difference Will This WORD Make In Me?

Your adversary, satan, challenges your authority because he has none, unless you play into his hand. Call his bluff this day! Declare God's Word over your life, knowing that God's active Word in your life keeps hell's agenda under your feet! Don't keep in step with what you feel. Move forward in what you KNOW! Walk on, Winning Warrior!

6

TO COME IN BETWEEN

Exodus 32:10 (GW)
"Now leave Me alone.
I'm so angry with them I am going to destroy them.
Then I'll make you into a great nation."

Did God just say, "LET ME ALONE NOW"?! Have you ever in your life fathomed such a thing?! But it's what God said! And I believe He meant it!

You see no matter how many times God stepped in to protect and provide for His people, no matter how far He separated these former slaves from captivity, God's freed ones kept imitating their captors! They looked just like the world around them and completely ignored the Generous God who delivered them. (Sounds vaguely familiar!)

As Moses experienced God's Glory on the mountaintop, God's people remaining at the bottom acted fifty-shades-of-crazy. A wild party broke out! Problem was, they partied in worship of dead gods (with a golden calf to boot!) while ignoring the One True God that had delivered them over and again. Jehovah championed their cause when nobody stood in line to help; yet in their liberation, they tossed Him like stale bread.

You've got to read Exodus 32, but for now, it went something like this . . . God essentially told Moses, *"I've been patient, but I'm done! I'm going to deal with them once and for all. I'll make a great nation out of you, Moses, but I'm going to take them out! Now let me alone to do it!"*

It takes a LOT to push this patient God to the brink, but the jig was up!

Stay with me; this is fascinating! Did you know that the word "intercessor" literally means, "to come in between"?

A Praying Person Comes In Between To Say, "God, You Have Every Right To Do This, But I Stand In The Gap Between You and This Situation Asking You to Reconsider."

Imagine that! God WANTS us to change His mind, to influence Him! Moses reminded Him: *"If you do this, the world will say you only brought them out here to take them out. Think what will happen to your reputation in the earth! And besides, you promised them by your OWN Name to multiply their generations. You don't break Your promises. I believe this!"*

Then, God did change His mind! He decided not to destroy them after all! (Exodus 32:14)

Friend, do you realize the privilege we possess to speak intimately to this All-Powerful God in such a way that we can actually influence how He responds?" FOR REAL!

When God said, "Let Me alone now," He was actually saying, "Moses, if you step aside, I'll act. But if you remain in between, I won't." Y'all, THIS IS THE POWER OF PRAYER!

God waits for true intercessors to come in between and remain! To stay there without letting go! To hold on UNTIL we see God move!

The Psalmist declared, "Because Abba bends down to listen, I will pray as long as I have breath!" (Psalm 116:2 NLT)

That's what Moses did! He prayed, urging God to reconsider . . . AND GOD DID!

What is going on in your living that needs your intercession? Where is it that you need to come in between?

God responds to the perpetual prayers of His people, those intercessors who stand in the gap, holding on with all they've got UNTIL they see God move! In fact, He's counting on the fact that you will! He delights to show mercy when we pray!

So what are we waiting for? Let's get to it! He's listening, you know!

What Difference Will This WORD Make In Me?

What is that area in your living that needs you to stand in the gap between that thing that has a mind of its own and God? Name it out loud. You cannot conquer a situation until you confront it in prayer. Spend this day declaring God's Word over this situation until it begins to look like God's Word! Believe that God delights in showing mercy . . . because HE DOES!

7

RUNNING THE RACE

Hebrews 12:1-3 (MSG)
"Strip down, start running—and never quit!
No extra spiritual fat, no parasitic sins.
Keep your eyes on Jesus,
who both began and finished this race we're in.
Study how He did it . . .
This will shoot adrenaline into your souls!"

Speaking of running, did you know the Boston Marathon draws the best runners from all over the world? Winning this contest establishes one runner as among the most elite contenders on the planet! Those top athletes focus on that prize and prepare for this endurance challenge like nothing else matters.

In 1980, Rosie Ruize became the first woman in Boston Marathon history to cross the finish line. Imagine the thunderous applause as officials placed the wreath on her head! In the following hours, people started questioning this Cinderella story. How did she achieve this famous distinction without anyone even knowing her name?

Then, folks started noticing sagging cellulite on her legs. The other competitors began comparing notes. They realized that no one saw her running throughout the 26.2-mile course.

The truth came out: this phony athlete jumped into the race in the last stretch! *WHAT THE WORLD?!!!* You can fake some things but camouflaging as a top marathon runner? Now that's a whole other level!

Unbelievably, the bogus runner refused to admit she cheated! She even offered to run another marathon just to prove herself. Of course, that never happened.

After several sit-downs, interviewers concluded that this pretend runner genuinely believed she ran the race and won. She lied convincingly, divorced from all sense of reality.

Friend, this Faith journey is a marathon, not a sprint. It requires discipline. It necessitates a steadfastness that refuses to quit when life throws curveballs.

I can't help but consider "believers in Jesus" who can talk (and post) like they are smackdab in the middle of the race. Problem is, no one ever sees them running!

Oh, they attend church once in a blue moon (some not even that!) but there's no personal investment whatsoever. Pretend believers occasionally participate in things that make them feel connected to the race. But they have no follow-through when no one is looking except God Himself.

Some of us are squeezing our cheeks right now. We feel the "Ouch!" that comes from looking into the mirror of God's Word, realizing we need some adjustments. (I get you!) But isn't it wonderful that He loves us enough to show us where we veer off course? God wants the blessed life for us more than we want it for ourselves!

God Knows If We Only Talk About The Race Without Actually Running It, We'll Panic When Hard Times Press Us! If We Develop No Training To Overcome The Obstacles, We'll Quit!

We know we are NOT made for the sidelines! It's just sometimes easier to merely talk about the race than to run it!

Y'all! We get no prize without the process! How we feed our faith when no one is watching directly determines our authenticity when everyone is watching.

I desperately long to echo the Apostle Paul's words as he inched closer to that glorious finish line:

*"This is the only race worth running. I've run hard right
to the finish, believed all the way.
All that's left now is the shouting—
God's applause! Depend on it, He's an honest judge.
He'll do right not only by me,
but by everyone eager for His coming."
(2 Timothy 4:7-8 MSG)*

If you're reading this, I believe your heart cries for it too. Let us determine TODAY to do more than talk about the race or even look like a runner. Let's RUN!

What Difference Will This WORD Make In Me?
Read these verses again. Carve out some time today to get alone with God. Feed your Faith. Train your mind. Do something that helps you RUN STRONG AND SURE IN GOD!

8

UNIQUE AND USEFUL

Jeremiah 18:1-6 (MSG)
"God told Jeremiah, "Up on your feet!
Go to the potter's house.
When you get there, I'll tell you what I have to say."
So I went to the potter's house, and sure enough,
the potter was there, working away at his wheel.
Whenever the pot the potter was working on turned
out badly, as sometimes happens
when you are working with clay,
the potter would simply start over
and use the same clay to make another pot.
Then God's Message came to me:
"Can't I do just as this potter does?" God's Decree!
"Watch this potter. In the same way
That this potter works his clay, I work on you!"

When I buy new appliances, I usually toss the instructions and settle for a YouTube instructional video. Watching someone else demonstrate the specifics clicks better in my own noggin.

God deposited revelation into Jeremiah for the sake of the people. But Jeremiah struggled to ingest the magnitude of all God was saying. So, the Lord said, "Let's take a field trip!"

God directed Jeremiah to a location as common to us as a grocery store. Everyone in that day knew the local potter's whereabouts. Without clay pots, one's hands were the only containers available!

Each pot has its own flair. The artisan creates each piece unique AND useful!

Despite the potter's excellent craftmanship, sometimes the clay proves its imperfection. It begins to do its own thing which cripples its usefulness. If left to itself, it becomes good for nothing. (Sounds harsh but it's true!)

So, what does the potter do?

The potter doesn't walk off in a huff, leave the flawed clay to its own demise, or toss it on the trash heap. Instead, the potter sticks with this weak vessel and starts the process over, molding and shaping this lump into something unique AND useful all over again.

We're Clay Pots, Y'all!
Without The Potter's Touch, We're Lumps!
But When He Lays His Hand On Us . . .
We Become a Creation Both Breathtakingly
Unique and Extraordinarily Useful!

Because we are rebels to the core, our self-centeredness predictably demands to have its way. The aftershock inevitably breaks us and all that matters to us.

As we become full of ourselves, we eventually lie broken, feeling good for nothing.

Yet despite our nonsense, God refuses to leave us to our own demise. He doesn't give up on us even though we give up on Him. He doesn't toss what is tainted or bury what is blemished. God simply melts this flawed, failing clay for the sake of remaking us yet again.

Let's be honest. The melting and remaking are momentarily painful. In fact, they can prove extremely uncomfortable. But oh, the beauty this clay pot becomes, the bounty it carries!

I'm in complete awe of this God that owns it all, yet no matter how many times our selfishness gets in the way, chooses to stick with what He started. He sees His Work through to its completion no matter how many times our pride takes the wheel!

God said to Jeremiah and He says to YOU this day, "I began a good work in you and I am faithful to complete it no matter how long it takes and how many times we start again. You are My Masterpiece and I think you're worth it!" (Philippians 1:6; Ephesians 2:10)

What Difference Will This WORD Make In Me?
No matter where you stand or the mess you've made, know that The Father refuses to forsake you. Choose this day to get back on the potter's wheel and let Him finish the good work that He began in YOU! It's NOT too late!

9

FOR THE LOVE OF HIM

Psalm 16:11 (NLT)
"You will show me the way of life,
granting me the joy of Your Presence
and the pleasures of living with You forever."

What place recalibrates you and helps your heart find center? What dwelling warms your soul from the cold and rekindles life into you again?

Of all the places Jesus traveled in His earthly ministry, I don't know of any home He loved to visit more than that special place in Bethany...the home of Lazarus, Martha, and Mary.

Droves of locals surely wanted Jesus to stay with them for at least one of His stopovers. But He always chose to rest and refresh Himself in the company of these three intimate friends.

Crowds clamored for the Messiah every hour of the day because they heard He had healed people, offered deliverance to tormented souls, even multiplied loaves and fish to meet people's needs. All their reasons for wanting close proximity to this Miracle Worker wouldn't fit on a page! But think about it. When Jesus walked through the doors of His true friends, they refused to press Him for this healing or that provision. Instead, they honored the Messiah's Presence in their midst and remained in awe that He chose to spend time with them.

I can imagine Lazarus saying, "Please come sit where it's comfortable." Martha would say something like, "When is the last time you ate? Let me fix dinner for you." Mary probably whispered, "You've been pouring yourself out all day. We need nothing more than to just sit right here with You."

These lovers of Jesus wanted nothing FROM Him except the joy of His Presence. It was all "For the Love of HIM!"

THIS set their home apart from the rest. These friends didn't clobber Him with petitions. They esteemed most highly the PERSON of God over the PROVISIONS of

God. They deeply longed to dwell where His very Presence enveloped the room.

Of course, the Lord NEEDS nothing. But I promise you this…He WANTS to be with those who reciprocate His love. He longs to be with those who yearn to simply dwell intimately right where He is.

This is important! I'm *not* saying that Jesus does not delight in meeting our needs. My goodness, HE DOES! But oh, if we could comprehend the magnitude of all that is available to us when we linger in His Presence, Friend, we would find everything we need RIGHT THERE where He is.

When we long just to remain where He remains, we cannot help but bump smackdab into healing and provision. Miracles happen without Him having to speak a word. His very Presence makes the impossible now possible!

As We Seek The Father's Heart More Than His Hand, The Spirit Of The Living God Infuses Us With All We Need AND THEN SOME!

And get this, as we draw near and bask in His Presence, the Lord realigns every aspect of us. We walk away visibly different. When we've gazed long into His eyes, others who look into our eyes know we've been with the One whose eyes are like fire. And before it's all over with, they'll want that fire in their eyes, too.

Oh, to live "For the Love of HIM!"

What Difference Does This WORD Make In Me?
Let's practice His Presence today. Shelve your personal needs and challenges. Don't ask for anything. Whew, that's not easy if we typically pray with our "to-do" list! But trust me, when we come and remain for the Love of the Father, God adds these other things as our portion. Our needs are met by Christ Jesus! I pinky promise, it's Truth!

10

WITHOUT CEASING. WHAT?!

1 Thessalonians 5:17 (NASB)
"Pray . . . without ceasing!"

Pray. Check!

Without ceasing. Come again?!

This cannot pertain to folks with families and jobs and...STUFF! How can it?

This directive was obviously written when people didn't juggle all that comes with modern living and technology. We've never been so busy! Surely God understands.

Speaking of technology, have you ever lost your phone? (Who hasn't?!) We usually don't get far before noticing. In fact, we stay so glued to this hand-held necessity that we lose it even as it's stuck to our ear in conversation! (Makes you feel stupid, huh?)

We check our phones so often that every spare moment lures us back into that screen. The time we lose weekly to this device has grown so exponentially that phone carriers send us reports to help monitor our use.

Imagine for a moment if we engaged our conversation with God like we engage our cell phones. What if we spoke to Him in every spare moment? What if we wore a contraption on our wrist that vibrated continuously to redirect our attention back to God? What if we felt so compelled to stay connected to this ongoing conversation with the Lover of our soul that we dare not leave home without it?

What if we rushed to fix things when something is not working properly in this exchange, like we do the minute our phones glitch? (YOU KNOW YOU FREAK OUT!!)

What if, instead of looking at our screen when we roll over, we talked to God first and listened attentively for His whisper toward us? What if we then checked in every few minutes with such mindfulness of His Presence throughout the day. WHAT IF?!!

What if we recharged our souls as intentionally as we recharge our phones? What if, when we needed answers, we talked to the One who knows ALL things instead of defaulting to Google that tells us only what media moguls curate?

You're likely thinking what I'm thinking... *OUCH! This stings!* (Remember, it stung me first!)

This idea to "pray without ceasing" sounds so unreasonable until you realize we practice this "without ceasing" every day, just with our technology instead of the One who stays faithful to us even when we live faithless toward Him.

"Pray without ceasing." It's not as difficult or complicated as we like to make it. It simply means we pray without drawing to a close. We converse with the One who knows us best and loves us most before our feet hit the floor. Then we just keep engaging this amazing Father. We keep picking up the chat throughout the day like we're never finished. In fact, we let conversation with Jesus become the very last words of our day. There is no conclusion; it just keeps going!

Another way to think of it... "Make your life a prayer." (1 Thess. 5:17 tPt)

What If We Made Our Whole Lives A Prayer, Without A Finale?
What If We Stayed So Attuned To His Voice That Every Other Voice Took A Back Seat?

THIS is the blessed life God designed for us. THIS is the holy habit that provides GPS navigation for every situation in every season with wisdom found nowhere else.

Let's try it today. Let's practice "praying without ceasing" until it becomes our holy habit!

What Difference Will This WORD Make In Me?
It may sound awkward, but let's set reminders on our phones for each hour of this day. Let it jog our memory to Praise God for His goodness. Let's tell Him what He means to us.

Listen for His prompting in your soul. You may not FEEL Him initially but if you keep going in God, I promise you, it'll become a holy habit that changes EVERYTHING in your living! FOR REAL!

11

THE TROJAN HORSE OF THE HEART

Ephesians 4:27 (AMPC)
*"Leave no room or foothold for the devil
[give no opportunity to him]."*

You remember the famous Trojan Horse narrative, right?

After many years of defeat in war, the Greeks signaled surrender to Troy and offered their opponent a massive wooden horse. They rolled the "gift" to Troy's city gates before departing.

Some leaders urged Troy to refuse it. Others shoved the massive horse inside the city walls, then reveled in their victory well into the night.

When Troy eventually slumbered from their partying, forty enemy soldiers emerged from within the horse, then opened wide the city's gates for the Greek armies to enter and destroy!

The enemy slashed the throats of Troy's mighty soldiers while their senses were dulled in the dark. This once-impenetrable city found itself at the enemy's disposal and leveled in one day!

Y'all! God's Breathing WORD today is branding this upon our hearts! *Don't offer the enemy any opportunity to manipulate you!*

When you study this verse's context, you realize the deceiver finds his easiest access most often through our emotions.

Satan Finds His Footing Through Our Feelings. When Spiritual Senses Dull And Fluctuating Feelings Heighten, Hell Wins!

The enemy of our soul surveys the territory of our lives, looking for opportunities to compromise the gates of our soul through our reactions. From there, he gets the run of the place and destroys us from within!

When do our feelings heighten to the point that our spiritual stamina diminishes? Where does the enemy find his footing because we momentarily lose ours?

The deceiver finds these openings in times of deep disappointment, in seasons of offense, and in those moments when we fear people's rejection more than we crave God's approval. (Read these three "Trojan horses" again and consider such moments in your own story.)

Certainly, we recall when disappointment laid heavy on us. Our capacity to hear God collapsed beneath disappointment's sting, and our emotions heightened to dangerous levels. Did our reaction offer our adversary an opportunity?

Surely, we remember when an excruciating wound festered into an offense that lured us right into the enemy's trap. (I'm raising my hand!)

We all have those moments when others' opinions of us completely eclipse what God speaks over us and into us!

THESE, my friend, THESE moments, hell slithers in to find his footing because we have temporarily lost ours.

I know. You feel completely justified in your reaction to this hard place you face. You can list reasons why no part of this is fair. Listen! You can be right and still be wrong! Being right has nothing to do with it! Stop validating your reasons for carrying disappointment, offense, or concern about what others think. Giving the enemy access to your soul will bury you, no matter who's right!

I'm not casting blame or shame, I promise. I'm simply trying to awaken us to the nature of hell's strategies. This deceiver seeking our destruction waits patiently to get inside our souls and wreak havoc on all that matters to us. A foothold today becomes a stronghold tomorrow. And once hell holds us strongly, he has no intention of letting go! He calls the shots, and we become his puppets! (That's no exaggeration!)

What are you carrying today that makes room for the enemy to find an access point? What is festering in your soul and poisoning YOU while others run free?

I declare THIS day that your heart senses freedom from this foothold that has become a stronghold! Refuse to stay stuck. Kick that Trojan horse out, get your eyes off the pain and on the One who desires to heal you from the inside out! As you fix your face like flint upon the One who is already opening doors for your next, every entanglement breaks off you! He's setting you free, and not just free, but FREE INDEED!

Now walk…better yet, RUN, like you're free!

What Difference Will This WORD Make In Me?
Refuse to rehearse the pain for even one more day. Choose to recite God's Word over your life with expectancy that He holds the keys to your next!

12

WHEN DISAPPOINTMENT LAYS HEAVY

John 16:33b (PHILLIPS)
*"You will find trouble in the world—but,
never lose heart, I have conquered the world!"*

I've never met one person who hasn't faced real disappointment. Jesus outright told us that we're not home yet, and on this side of Heaven, we will run smackdab into trouble. He also said not to lose heart because He has already conquered what seeks to conquer us!

Disappointment...it's the distance between expectation and experience. Sometimes it's a gap. Sometimes it's a Grand Canyon! How we handle that chasm determines WHETHER we move forward and WHO we become on the other side. Our tendency in seasons of deep disappointment is to withdraw, unconsciously, from people, or even from God.

Don't believe me?

In 1911, Swiss psychologist Édouard Claparède treated a 47-year-old patient with no short-term memory. At the beginning of each appointment, they shook hands. After a few sessions, for her next visit, the doctor concealed a pin in his palm. As they shook hands, she felt the sharp pain and immediately withdrew her hand.

Moments later, this patient recalled nothing of the puncture. Yet, from then on, she refused to shake the doctor's hand. Without understanding why, she no longer trusted him. Her response to pain lingered though her memory of it did not. (R. Gregory ed., The Oxford Companion to the Mind (1987) p. 21)

We Can Carry The Residue Of Pain That Causes Us To Unconsciously Tap The Brakes Of Our Faith. We Stop Reaching Toward God's Hand That Keeps Reaching Toward Us!

Disappointment can become discouragement. Discouragement, left untouched by God's Power, metastasizes into Despair. Each of these can allow the enemy of our soul to get inside and poison our trust reservoir with God.

Let's face it…we get disappointed when it FEELS like God "missed it". Oftentimes, it is really we who missed Him! But no matter what it FEELS like in this moment, God cannot miss! If we do not guard our gates, it's GAME OVER!

Here are seven tangible ways to combat deep disappointment and emerge stronger, sturdier, surer than you were on the front side. It's not impossible! In fact, it's proof that the God of IMPOSSIBLE is surely at work in you!

1. Don't Be Surprised by Disappointment; Expect it!
Life is never going to feel fair. This reality doesn't change God's goodness! He's good at being good! He's good at being good TO YOU and ME!

2. Step Back from That Situation Trying to Swallow You Whole!
Pain is greedy. It demands more and more of you until you sense only its sting.

3. Choose to Praise God with a Sound Contrary to Your Situation!

Elevating HIM higher than "it" pulls disappointment down! Take disappointment off the Throne; put God back in His rightful place!

4. Declare God's Word Over Your Life!

WORD yourself! God's Word LIFTS you from that pain trying to overwhelm you. You're passing through!

5. Find beauty in your life right now amid the ashes! It's there!

Your focus determines your future. Magnifying the beauty minimizes the ashes!

6. Pour Oil on Your Situation.

As tears flow, choose to anoint that pain with FRESH OIL that resurrects what feels dead inside you! It empowers you to say, "Surely God is Here in THIS place Giving Me Power with God and Favor with Men!"

7. Reach Beyond Yourself! Refuse to Isolate No Matter How Much Your Flesh Screams for It!

When I get in a dark hole, if I try to pull myself out, I fall back in. But when I look outside my situation and encourage someone else, it lifts me out, too. If I start talking into YOUR head, I get myself out of MY head. When I REACH OUT instead of trying to CLIMB OUT . . . I GET OUT!

What Difference Will This WORD Make In Me?

Make a promise with yourself and with God that you will put these seven things into practice for the next seven days! See what God will do!

13

DEALING WITH OUR JOSEPH AND BENJAMIN

Acts 3:19 (tPt)
*"And now you must repent and turn back to God
so that your sins will be removed,
And so that times of refreshing will stream
from the Lord's Presence."*

We all have people in our living that arouse discord within us. Our days run smoother when they are completely out of the picture. (Don't act like you don't know what I'm talking about!)

Remember the story of Joseph's brothers, who loathed him so much they tossed him into a pit then left him to die? (Genesis 37) They concocted a tall tale to cover their own tails! They transferred the blood on their own hands to Joseph's coat, convincing their dad a wild animal had devoured his favorite son.

Years later, in a desperate condition, the brothers traveled to Egypt to find food. Famine had devastated their entire household. They could not know that the very brother they had tried to destroy would now determine whether they would live or die! Joseph had miraculously risen through the ranks, from Egypt's slave to second-in-power over all the land.

As Joseph looked into the eyes of those who sought his demise, he realized one brother was unaccounted for. The guilty brothers had left their baby brother, Benjamin, at home. (They had no use for Joseph OR Benjamin. Both were Daddy's favorites.)

Believe it or not, these dudes STILL didn't recognize their brother. It never occurred to them that Joseph could still be alive.

This second-in-command offered to feed them, but ONLY after they returned with Benjamin.

Imagine with me. It's been twenty-two years since these brothers abandoned Joseph in a pit to die, and even longer since they started carrying animosity toward Benjamin, too. But that jig was up! If they didn't deal with their issues concerning the ones they loathed, they would die!

Friends, Unless We Allow God To Work In Our Hearts, We Will Struggle With Destructive Sensitivities For Years...Decades...A Lifetime. This Junk Metamorphoses Into Deep-Rooted Animosity That Sours Our Soul.

Mind you, these emotions are not benign. They multiply! They steal from us so much that God has dreamed for our living!

I cannot tell you how many times in years of ministry that I've watched folks rob themselves of SO MUCH God has for them because they refused to deal with their animosity toward their Joseph and Benjamin. They fought to hang on to that resentment. Consequently, they missed out on provisions and promotions God had waiting just for them. (Read Joseph's story! He refused to let bitterness find a home in him. Consequently, God promoted him to high places!)

Folks, unless we know what to do with our Joseph and our Benjamin, we will not have food in the time of famine. Dealing with Joseph and Benjamin became the difference between life and death for those brothers' families and generations!

I know, I know. You may be thinking, "I can make peace with everyone EXCEPT...." But that's just it. There are no exceptions on this.

You may be entirely right about why that particular person doesn't deserve your peace toward them. But keeping score changes you, never them. It metastasizes into a thing that drives *you* further from God. So stop! "Repent...that times of refreshing will stream from the Lord's Presence" (Acts 3:19). Just do the right thing so all will be right and go right with you!

This decision doesn't let them off the hook. It lets YOU off the hook! Today is the day! TODAY!

What Difference Will This WORD Make In Me?

Who is your Joseph, your Benjamin? Name them. Refuse to rehearse all the reasons you feel justified in your frustration toward them. Make up your mind THIS DAY that you are going to break out of that trapped place. First, pray for them. Then write an inbox, send a text... SOMETHING that speaks blessing into their lives. You don't need to be best buds. But you do need to break a stronghold that's holding you strong. Once you've done this, Praise God throughout this day for the freedom we enjoy when He has the final Word in our living!

14

ANXIETY: IT'S JUST THE SYMPTOM

Isaiah 35:4 (NIV)
*"Say to those with fearful hearts,
'Be strong, do not fear; YOUR GOD WILL COME!'"*

Anxiety is more poisonous than we imagine. But we carry this devastator so continuously that we become accustomed to its dogged grip! Over time, even low-grade fear wreaks havoc on every part of our constitution from the inside out!

This disease exposes the obvious truth that things have not turned out the way we once imagined for ourselves. This is NOT AT ALL the life we dreamed of! But where did we change course? How did we swerve so subtly that we did not even discern it?

We could throw a thousand little reasons on the board to justify where we find ourselves, but I dare say our barrage of blame would uncover mere symptoms. To get to the crux of the matter, we must shovel straight to the root system.

This chronic low-grade anxiety, that sometimes detonates into full-fledged panic, reveals that, somewhere along the way, we stopped wholeheartedly believing God's unconditional affection toward us. (It sounds simple, but it's oh so true!)

It means that, at some point on the journey, I lost absolute confidence that God is everything He says He is TO ME and that He does everything He says He does FOR ME! I lost certainty that the God who made me for Himself actually longs to intimately relate to me daily, steering me into blessing I could never find on my own!

As we pull up the root, we find the culprits. First, we ever so subtly drifted from ferociously feeding our faith. It didn't seem like a big deal, did it? But it surely took its toll.

Second, we harbor deep disappointment from situations that didn't turn out at all the way we envisioned. The emotional aftershock lays heavy while questions linger in the silence.

The drifting and the disappointment squelch every ounce of wonder that once-upon-a-time lived large in us. (You know it's true!)

Do you ever allow yourself to just hang out in God's unrelenting love for you? In the deepest parts of you, do you truly believe that He tenderly embraces you right where you are, yet loves you too much to leave you there?

When We Don't Wholeheartedly Trust God's Heart Toward Us, We'll Never Really Trust Him With ANY Part Of Us!

We'll lose our confidence in Him, and consequently in ourselves too, one breath at a time, until it's all gone.

This Everlasting Father delights in you today! Refuse to allow distractions, drifting, or even disappointment to rob you of experiencing His absolute delight toward you. Each of these thieves steal from you the very reason you live and breathe . . . to love and be loved.

There's nothing colder than a cold heart, frozen in worry and unbelief. That's not your story today! Breathe Him in! He sings over you and smiles at the very thought of you! Yes, I'm talking to YOU!

What Difference Will This WORD Make In Me?

Jot down the top three situations that feed into the anxiety in your heart right now. Now consider some of the Names and attributes of God that speak to these situations and fuel your confidence that our Good Father is ridiculously superior to these momentary situations that threaten to swallow you. Compared to The Author and Finisher of your story, what you face is no match for what you carry when you carry HIM! This Doting Father adores you. He fights for you...and He always wins!

15

SO, YOU NEED WISDOM?

Proverbs 1:7 (AMP)
*"The [reverent] Fear of the Lord is
the beginning and the preeminent part of wisdom
[its starting point and its essence]."*

Who doesn't need wisdom...by the boatload...EVERY SINGLE DAY?!! Stepping into my mornings, in mere seconds I see more evidence that people have lost their ever-loving minds! They've tossed aside wisdom for some bogus pseudo-intelligence that collapses at the first hint of testing.

Every minute, social media platforms bombard us with an inundation of information. (Mostly, this "information" contrives calculated falsehoods that mock wisdom.)

We get every kind of option for every kind of scenario. The decisions and the noise seem endless.

If we don't know what we stand for, we'll fall for anything! We desperately need wisdom! But wisdom is not mere textbook knowledge. It's more than the opinions of those who have gone before us. Wisdom is altogether different because it derives from someONE altogether "other" …God Himself!

If you need wisdom, our Generous God says, "ASK!" (James 1:5) He thrills to give us what we need. But get this:

If Our View Of God Is Out Of Whack, Our Capacity To Carry Wisdom Will Be Too!

We must continually re-evaluate how we see the One who is superior to ALL things in ALL of time and space, or His wisdom will be lost on us!

"Fearing the Lord" is not about dread or terror. It's altogether different.

Problem is, we've heard of God's ALL-Knowing and ALL-Powerful essence so continuously that we've lost all reverential astonishment at His Majesty and Splendor!

Mere words should fall short as we try to describe HIM. Yet we strut in our own sufficiency with hearts numbed and senses dulled to the absolute "otherness" of this Unconquerable God!

Who are we that this Magnificent God is even mindful of us? Why should He give us the time of day? (Psalm 8)

Why do we fear everything EXCEPT God? You know it's true! (This reveals how outrageously diminished our view of Jesus is!)

The beginning of Wisdom is NOT the fear of failure, NOT the fear of the enemy seeking to destroy you, NOT the fear of others' opinions or rejection. It is NOT fear over our finances or the future.

THE BEGINNING OF WISDOM IS THE FEAR OF THE LORD!!!

My heart breaks as I peruse the landscape of the American Church. Many "believers" say they love Jesus but live shockingly incongruent to Jesus' Infallible Word. They stand *for* what Jesus emphatically stands *against*, and *against* what Jesus outrightly stands *for*. What happened?!!!!

It all comes down to this: Many people love Jesus, but very few fear Him. Remember…If our fear of God is out of whack, our capacity to wield wisdom will be, too!

Listen friend, until we fear the LORD, the enemy will never fear us. The enemy will never tremble in our presence until we tremble in God's Presence! Can we mean it when we say, *"I only tremble at Your Word!" (Isaiah 66:2)*?

If we fear God, we will never need to fear anything else!

What FEELS so big in your life right now? You may think you need a thousand other things to remedy this situation. I'm telling you, more than anything, you need the wisdom only God can give. As we elevate reverential fear of the Lord into its rightful place in our hearts, Wisdom will be our portion! As we discern Christ's true Might and Magnificence, that problem we face loses its power to keep us up at night because thoughts of Jesus' Supremacy will!

What Difference Will This WORD Make In Me?

Jot down the problem that seems so large and in charge. Then begin to jot down facets of The Supreme One that overpower that which seeks to overpower you!

I decree this insurmountable mountain will become a mole hill! God will give you everything you need to scale it! You will no longer tremble at this perplexity. You will tremble only at His Word, then walk across the rubble of that leveled mountain!

16

EYES FORWARD

Philippians 3:12-14 (MSG & NLT)

"I'm not saying that I have this all together, that I have it made. But I am well on my way, reaching out for Christ, who has so wondrously reached out for me. (MSG) I have not achieved it [perfection], but I focus on this one thing: Forgetting the past and looking forward to what lies ahead, I press on to reach the end of the race and receive the Heavenly prize for which God, through Christ Jesus, is calling us." (NLT)

Have you driven anywhere lately? How often did you use your rearview mirror? How much of your focus remained glued to the windshield? To be sure, your forward focus got you to the intended spot!

It's completely nonsensical to imagine reaching our destination while focused on that tiny mirror that reveals only what is behind us. Even small children understand this concept . . . to get where we're going, we must focus forward.

Yet how often do we fixate on what magnifies our past? Even if we don't converse about those things behind us, we certainly internally rehearse them entirely too often. In fact, if truth be told, so much of the junk back there deeply impacts decisions right here. (You know it's true!)

What is it, back there? Perhaps it's a wound that still bleeds when bumped. Maybe it's poor choices with bitter outcomes that haunt your living.

We all could dissect a myriad of situations and seasons we could have, should have handled differently. But folks . . . we will not get where we're going by studying that rearview mirror. To fully live this gift called life, WE MUST SET OUR GAZE FORWARD!

It Is NOT The Plan Of God To Wallow In The Misery Of Regret.
It Is NOT The Plan Of God To Remain Fixated On Past Pain That Only Puts You Deeper In A Pit of Defeat.

The Apostle Paul knew a thing or two about regrets. He's the guy who tried to murder Christians before he became one. This dude once hunted down believers in Jesus. Then *he* got hunted down for believing in Jesus. Talk about whiplash!

This man lived in deep regret for snuffing out beautiful lives that adored the LORD he came to adore.

Can you imagine the memories that tormented this man of God each evening as he closed his eyes to rest? When the room went dark, his mind followed suit. No matter how much he had gotten right, in that moment it never felt like enough to overwhelm what he had gotten so wrong. The night grew outrageously loud in his head. (Can anyone relate?)

But Paul finally made up his mind that all his energies, all his focus belonged to the race set before him. He determined to run with eyes forward toward Jesus and forget anything that lingered behind him. He realized that where God was taking him was so much bigger than where he had been.

Friend, WHERE GOD LONGS TO TAKE YOU IS SO MUCH BIGGER THAN WHERE YOU'VE BEEN!

So let us forget to remember the past. Yes, that's what I said . . . *forget to remember*!

Stop rehearsing what's behind you! The rehashing of that thing is a trap!

When Jesus is the LORD of our living, the Omniscient One who knows all things decides to forget our past. It's time for us to forget it too.

Daily determine to carry a short memory and a clear direction.

Choose to fix your eyes and fasten your heart to the future God has dreamed for you! It's the only way out of your regret. It's the only way forward!

What Difference Will This WORD Make In Me?

As you consider that part of your past that keeps tripping you up, lay it before the Lord (even if you've done it a thousand times before.) Ask for forgiveness if you need to. Offer forgiveness to that one who wounded you so badly. Get up from this place believing that God's dream for your living is so much bigger than anything behind you in that tiny mirror. Walk through this day with your eyes forward and focus on living FULLY ALIVE in the assignment God has for you!

17

GOD IS NOT SLOW!

Hebrews 10:23 (AMP)
*"Let us seize and hold tightly the confession
of our hope without wavering,
for He who promised is reliable and trustworthy
and faithful [to His Word]."*

Since time began, God has been fulfilling His Promise
to bring us back home to Him. Matthew meticulously
outlined the genealogy of Jesus Christ to show us that
this has always been God's Plan! Matthew reminds us
that Jesus Christ is the Son of David and the son of
Abraham. (1:1)

God's People thought He was slow to the draw on, or
even forgetful of, all He previously prophesied through
His Prophets. They assumed He must surely be

preoccupied with more pressing things. Yet as they doubted privately and complained publicly, the promise was perpetually in progress.

The Lord was laying the groundwork, carefully hand-selecting the folks through whom He would reveal the Promised One. Every detail of this precisely planned story was pointing us closer to that climatic moment in history when the Word became flesh and made Himself at home among us. (Read it again, and slowly. Ponder each word. We've heard it so often that we've lost the absolute shock and awe of this reality!)

Divinity Became Dirt, AND HE CHOSE IT . . . JUST TO GET US BACK TO HIM!

Y'all! Our God doesn't just know the end from the beginning, He meticulously positions every detail to make that specific moment ripe and ready for His Promise in our stories. Our Good, Good Father is ALWAYS moving toward that appointed time to fulfill His Promise to in your journey and mine!

Are WE?!!!

There is ALWAYS so much more at work than what we can see. Just because we cannot discern it does not mean it is not there! Our God is careful and deliberate, but friend . . . our God is never slow!

Lord, remind us when we forget . . . You are ALWAYS in the process of keeping Your Promise over our living. You are moving when we sense You and when we don't. Let us not be slow to embrace Your Word over our living with Great Faith and steadfast obedience. You are not slow so let us not be slow either! Your Promise for us is better than we deserve and so much better than we imagine! We love you and stand in awe of you, our Magnificent Promise Keeper!

What Difference Will This WORD Make In Me?
What of your living feels stalled? Name it! In fact, walk through this day declaring Hebrews 10:23 over that piece of your story. Encourage yourself in the Lord until any doubt disappears and God's Promise-in-progress saturates your thoughts this day! He is not slow to the draw! He's active in your living this very day!

18

PHANTOM FEAR

1 Peter 5:8 (NLT)
*"Stay alert! Watch out for your great enemy, the devil.
He prowls around like a roaring lion,
looking for someone to devour."*

I'm no wildlife expert, but even I know gazelles lope like lightning! Did you realize a gazelle can sprint up to 60 miles per hour?! That's twice as fast as any human on record. (I looked it up!)

In fact, only cheetahs have what it takes to surpass gazelles. But even these bad boys rarely devour gazelles, because gazelles outwit them. They change directions lightning-fast during the chase to destabilize the cat's speed. (Genius!)

Besides that, gazelles possess endurance that leaves cheetahs in their dust. It's easy-peasy to outlast their stalker.

It's safe to say gazelles carry an unfair advantage against most predators in the wild. Not even the king of the jungle can touch them...or, can he?

Gazelles often race together. But get this, if a gazelle catches a glimpse of a lion staring her down from the bushes as the herd sprints by, that terrorizing glare can halt the swifter one dead in her tracks!

This creature with the capacity to outrun, outwit, AND outlast the predator stands paralyzed by phantom fear. The lion's intimidation settles on that isolated one like a straitjacket. Then that enemy doesn't have to lift a single claw!

The swift-hoofed gazelle moving with the pack had no reason to freeze, no reason to fear the lesser one. But when her feet stilled and her fear skyrocketed, she actually emboldened her enemy to make her worst fears become reality! Her tomorrows...devoured!

Listen friend, the enemy of your soul IS the lesser one! God has given you EVERYTHING you need to outwit, outlast, and completely overpower the one who prowls around LIKE a roaring lion. (His roar is so much bigger than his bite! He only wins if we let him!)

This enemy that seeks to terrorize and ultimately devour you has nothing going in his favor—unless you isolate yourself from those running in the same direction AND let your eyes lock onto his!

If You Are Moving In God And God Is Moving In You, The Enemy Cannot Catch You! He Cannot Outwit You, And He Surely Cannot Overpower You!

I don't know what you are facing in this season. But stay with the pack that outruns the enemy and keep running! Keep going in God! Run with fear if you must. Run with fright that makes your knees knock if you have to! But whatever you do, don't stop and surely don't stay. Just keep going in God! You carry the unfair advantage!

What Difference Will This WORD Make In Me?

Name the concern that has you paused. (It probably didn't take you long. You've been stuck there, paralyzed by the enemy's intimidation tactics.)

Get with someone this day who pushes you in God. Pray together! Speak God's Word over your situation, then run together like you know who wins! Leave the enemy in your dust!

19

THE PEACE OF GOD POUNDS TO A PULP

Romans 16:20 (tPt)
*"And the God of Peace will swiftly
pound satan to a pulp under your feet!
And the wonderful favor of our Lord Jesus
will surround you!"*

What comes to mind when you whisper, "Peace?" All my life, I've imagined a shelter. I envision standing in the middle of a perfect storm, yet finding a safe place to hide.

Indeed, there are those seasons in our living where God swoops us up and hides us in the cleft of the Rock and covers us with His hand. (Exodus 33:22) We are so hidden in God in that moment that the enemy cannot even find us. *(Now that's peace!)*

As I've survived some of those tumultuous tsunamis of life, I've also discovered that Peace is so much more than living on the defense. When true Shalom finds a home in us, it gives us the power to move on the offense.

In Scripture, "Peace" or "Shalom" is not merely shelter or safety. It actually denotes a straightening of what is bent. It signifies "wholeness," meaning, "the way it was created to be."

Are you getting this?!

**Real Peace Makes Right
What Has Gone Wrong!
It Says That Right In The Midst
of Our Brokenness God Can Mend And
Heal It "AS IT OUGHT TO BE!"**

As we consider today's verse, we'd be hard-pressed to find a defensive posture in play. God fully intends for His children to live in His high-definition Peace in such a way that this Peace swiftly pounds satan to a pulp! (I'd say that's emphatically offensive!)

Friends, we are not to hide out in this chaotic, contentious time waiting for the turmoil to subside. We are representatives of Christ in the earth. We walk in THAT authority and THAT power!

The God of Peace "will soon crush satan under His feet." The Greek word for "crush" resembles a smashing so completely beyond recognition to the object of the crushing.

Imagine stepping on a grape. You squish it into oblivion. THIS is the power to crush, and the Peace of God offers this power to US!

Friends, that's where hell belongs . . . under our feet! We are no match for satan or his schemes on our own; but in God, we have more than enough power to crush that enemy into oblivion.

"AND the wonderful favor of our Lord Jesus will surround you!" Oh Hallelujah! (Don't mind me! I'm just shouting over here!) Triumph . . . Victory . . . It belongs to US!

What Difference Will This WORD Make In Me?
What area in your living feels twisted and bent? Declare God's Word over that situation believing that "impossible" is not impossible to God! Praise Jesus like the bent thing is already straight. Worship Him like you believe with all that is in you that "it shall be as God intended" UNTIL you see it come to pass. UNTIL!

20

WHEN ALL HELL BREAKS LOOSE

Acts 12:5 (tPt)
*"The church went into a season
of intense intercession."*

When all hell breaks loose in your life, what is your initial reaction? I'm not asking what you want it to be. Truly, what is your "go to" reaction?

Do you ever pray because you know you're supposed to, but you don't actually expect God to answer? (I've done that!)

This thinking causes us to pray puny prayers, quick prayers, routine prayers that never stretch us and never change the situation.

When the Early Church got news that Peter (one of their generals) had been thrown into prison for his faith and faced execution at daylight, they gathered to pray.

They didn't look for God in a crisis moment. In fact, they didn't have to look FOR God at all; they had already been looking TO Him. They simply doubled down in their HABIT of prayer. (By the way, your habits direct your days and determine your destiny!)

The Passion Bible notes that the believers gathered and *"went into a season of intense intercession."* The Greek translation for "intense intercession" means *"to stretch tightly in prayer."*

If we truly want to see God move in our situations, we can't merely offer up to Him panicked prayers in our distress. It requires a stretching beyond familiarity. It necessitates exertion that thrusts us right out of our worn-out, practiced prayers.

Intercession that brings real change propels us into personal, uncharted waters. We determine to extend and expand ourselves beyond our usual capacity.

Nothing About "Intense Intercession" Is Casual Or Ordinary. We're Not Begging God To Change His Posture; The Stretching Is Actually Changing *OURS*! It's Changing *US*!

THIS is the kind of passionate prayer that broke through this impossibility the Early Church faced. Because of this intense intercession, Peter miraculously walked from that prison cell in a completely unexplainable way. (You have to read it! It's in Acts 12, and it's SO good! SO GOOD!)

This real story about real people trusting the only REAL GOD proves ALL OVER AGAIN that the Lord bends down low to listen to our prayers. It reminds us that He delights in stretching us to become more like whom He created us to be.

Together let us "stretch tightly in prayer." Let us choose to extend ourselves beyond our familiar, routine words that come out of our mouths on autopilot.

Let us lay our heart out before God and know that He cares about every detail. As we offer ourselves completely to Him, He offers Himself completely to us!

It's a beautiful thing! It's a powerful thing! It breaks the chains and causes captives to walk free! Just ask Peter!

What Difference will This WORD Make In Me?
As you pray today, determine to use brand new words. Allow no part of your time with the Lord to shift down into auto-pilot. Find different phrases to describe His Greatness and your devotion to all He is. STRETCH your vocabulary! Refuse to retreat to familiar prayers. Be bold enough to ask Him, "STRETCH ME, LORD!"

21

THE TIPPING POINT

Luke 13:18-19 (NLT)
Then Jesus said, "What is the Kingdom of God like?
How can I illustrate it?
It is like a tiny mustard seed that a man planted
in a garden [a small thing, a lesser thing!];
it grows and becomes a tree
[a large thing, a GREATER thing!],
and the birds make nests in its branches."

Is it just me, or are you feeling the weight of the hour too? So many significant things seem to be hanging in the balance. Governments and economies hang by a thread. Significant situations in our own lives feel increasingly fragile, too.

Our inability to squash the things that seek to squash us leaves us feeling small and weak. We lose steam, and the burden of it all makes us wonder why we keep trying. (If this is you, stay with me!)

Imagine for a moment that the daunting situation in your life sits on a scale. That dire circumstance hangs in the balance. No matter what you do, nothing changes. But hear me… that's only what it FEELS like.

In reality, every small step in the right direction draws us closer to the tipping point of that scale. In one moment, what once seemed impossible slides toward "possible!" (Y'all! Every step in God's direction tilts you closer to "possible!")

Something that once seemed lesser now becomes GREATER! The situation incrementally gains momentum until the result becomes unstoppable! You discover the breaking point. Actually, YOU DISCOVER THE *BREAKTHROUGH* POINT! (Big difference!)

Is this clicking in you yet?!

A Tipping Point Is That Watershed Moment Which Alters The Trajectory Of A Thing. Something That Once Teetered In The Balance Now Takes Off In Your Favor And Overtakes The Obstacle That Stood In Your Way.

Speaking of something small that takes off and cannot be reversed…let's talk 'mustard seed'. It's one of the tiniest seeds in all of the botanical world. In fact, it's smaller than a speck of pepper. For real! It would seem powerless to fight even a flea. YET, once this tiny but mighty seed takes root, it gradually inches toward that tipping point where it cannot be destroyed! (I'm telling you the truth!!!)

Once that infinitesimal seed reaches that breakthrough moment, you can try stomping it down, burning it out, even tearing it up. Have at it! It's not going anywhere!

And get this: once that tiny seed hits that threshold, it aggressively takes out everything in its way. This minuscule mustard seed is the most feared plant in all of Israel because once it reaches that tipping point, it becomes indestructible!

Are we connecting the dots? God is essentially saying, "When your Faith is in ME...not your skills, or experience, or connections...when your heart is wholly fixed on the King and His Kingdom...THEN look out because breakthrough is coming! No matter what it looks like in this moment, as you keep acting in Faith...your tipping point hastens. And from there, you take out the thing that tried to take out you!"

Friends, just as the mustard seed grows strong, secure, and able to withstand all conditions, God desires that your Faith in Him become that unstoppable!

Keep taking that next step. Keep believing even when nothing seems different. Keep trusting when you want to quit.

Step of Faith...by step of Faith...you inch closer to that tipping point when the Faith inside you becomes indestructible in all seasons and situations. From that place, all God has spoken over your life comes to pass and no one alive can stop it! Oh, Hallelujah!

What Difference Will This WORD Make In Me?

What step can you take this day, this hour, that hastens your tipping point? Make up your mind to put your Faith in action. MOVE in God's direction until your Faith is indestructible and your breakthrough is unstoppable!

22

NOT ASHAMED!

Romans 1:16 (VOICE)
"For I am not the least bit embarrassed about the gospel. I won't shy away from it, because it is God's Power to save EVERY person who believes."

What embarrasses you? (Like, has your kid ever blurted out questions to strangers like, "Why do you smell bad?" or "Where are your teeth?") We've all endured moments that make us want to crawl under the nearest table.

In ministry, I journey with folks through the grief of losing loved ones. Let me just say, every family has some crazy; when a loved one dies, that crazy tends to come out of the woodwork. Some individuals feel so ashamed of their family's shenanigans that they momentarily want to change their name. For real!

Life's pressure points expose issues hidden beneath the surface.

In The Pressing,
Whatever Is In You Comes Out!

In his second letter to Timothy, this Faith-general, the Apostle Paul, notes others' distancing from him. Friends left and right abandoned their leader who had introduced them to this most holy Faith. They feared any association with Paul.

You see, the Roman Empire hated the Church, but the emperor Nero especially despised Christians, so severely that he torched Rome then blamed God's People for it. He sought to recreate the city as a monument to himself, and scorned Christians became the scapegoat for his narcissism.

The masses swallowed the government's lie as fast as its mouthpieces propagated it. (Sound familiar?!) Consequently, brutal persecution against Christians spread like wildfire.

At the heart of it, folks' shame toward Paul was not really about Paul. Believers in Jesus stood at a crossroads. What they deeply believed about the Messiah was put to the test. This pressing revealed the real substance of the faith within them.

As Paul writes from prison, incarcerated in a cold, nasty, isolated dungeon because he refused to recant his Faith no matter the cost, He pours his heart out to young Timothy, urging, *"Never be ashamed of the testimony of our Lord, nor embarrassed over my imprisonment"* (2 Timothy 1:8) A few verses later, he pens, *"The confidence of my calling enables me to overcome every difficulty WITHOUT SHAME, for I have an intimate revelation of this God. And my faith in Him convinces me that He is MORE THAN ABLE to keep ALL I've placed in His Hands safe and secure until the fullness of His appearing."* (1:12)

Then Paul devastatingly names some fair-weathered friends who deserted him in that desperate hour. (Oh, the pain!) But he also mentions one devoted friend who stayed by his side: *"[He] never seemed to be ashamed of my chains."* (2 Timothy 1:16)

Paul was facing death with such courage. Yet realizing that some once-devoted comrades now ran for the hills because the going got tough . . . it surely stung like a thousand stings.

This committed soldier of Jesus finally determined in his soul, "If none go with me, STILL I will follow!"

Friends, it's getting crazy. Speaking up for the things of God will get you ostracized in some circles before you finish your first sentence. Hostility toward Jesus-lovers is escalating full-throttle.

If you believe God's Word is Ultimate Truth in every situation and season, rather than culture's latest ideas, you're labeled a hater of those who don't. But loving all people and agreeing with all their views are two completely different things. Too many Christians stay silent to avoid the turbulence.

But friends, "I am not *the least bit* embarrassed about the Gospel. *I won't shy away from it*, because it is God's Power to save EVERY person who believes." I'm shouting His Goodness and His Power in me from the rooftops! Won't you join me?

What Difference Will This WORD Make in Me?

Put your faith in action THIS DAY! Don't be afraid and surely don't be ashamed of the Gospel that transforms your life and your generations! Tell someone around you about Jesus (if you want to be super brave, tell several!) Testify of His Goodness. Brag on His Faithfulness. "Be strong and courageous! Do not be afraid or discouraged. For the Lord your God is with you wherever you go." (Joshua 1:9 NLT)

23

BREAK OUT OF THE HUDDLE

Matthew 5:14-16 (MSG)

"You're here to be light, bringing out the God-colors in the world. God is not a secret to be kept.
We're going public with this,
as public as a city on a hill.
If I make you light-bearers, you don't think I'm going to hide you under a bucket, do you? I'm putting you on a light stand. Now that I've put you there on a hilltop, on a light stand—SHINE! Keep open house; be generous with your lives.
By opening up to others, you'll prompt people to open up with God,
this generous Father in heaven."

Is anyone in your family a fan of football? Are we the only house that raises the TV volume so loud that our neighbors hear the play-by-play too?!

My husband has loved the Chicago Bears since he was a little guy running around in the backyard with towels in his shoulder pads to feel legit. He says Chicago is one of the last remaining old-school teams.

The Bears struggle mostly. My guy says they are "building right now". (He's been saying that for a decade!)

My husband occasionally travels to Soldier Field to watch the Bears on their home turf. The wind chill factor for one of those games hit nine degrees below zero. I STAYED HOME! I love him, but not that much!

Tickets for these games aren't cheap. Folks make tremendous investments of time and resources to attend one of these epic events. Fans thrill to witness players carry that ball down the field and dance a jig in the end-zone.

Sometimes in the midst of intense play, teams call a time-out. They huddle together to discuss their next move. It's strategic. It's necessary. It is right.

Imagine with me for a moment, though, that you traveled the distance, purchased the tickets, sat in those bone-chilling temps only to watch your team...*huddle*...for most of the game. WHAT?!! Nobody wants to pay those prices to watch eleven men stand thigh to thigh.

The crowd won't mind occasional huddles. They make the game better. But no one gathers to watch a closed circle; they come for some action!

What they really want to know, after the huddle, is...does it make a difference? When the players gather in private, does it positively affect the score in public? THIS is what matters!

Friends, belonging to a local body of believers is essential! Jesus repeatedly stressed the absolute need for His Church. I LOVE Christ's Church and would not want to live even a day without those blood-bought bonds Jesus died to give us.

But if we stay cocooned in our churches without breaking the huddle, crowds beyond our walls deem us irrelevant...and they are not wrong!

If We Don't Break Huddle And Go Public With This Extraordinary God Who Has Transformed Every Part Of Our Existence, Then We Are Missing The Point Entirely!

God's plan is for YOU and me to influence our neighbors and communities by His Light that shines in us. He fully intends for us to burn with such Light that others realize they were created to crave what we carry!

Folks, the only reason you and I get to live this life of Faith is because SOMEBODY shined HIM in our presence. They lived a life that made us hungry for that same life-altering Love and Light!

I love time in the huddle. Those are MY People! MY Tribe! But if we are to accomplish God's assignment upon our living, we MUST go public with this transforming Faith. Let us live so that we get to dance in the end-zone with *others* who find Him because we chose to shine in a world gone dark!

What Difference Will This WORD Make In Me?

Do something out of your box today! Break out of the huddle and score publicly in a way that surprises even you. Someone's life depends upon your boldness and your obedience this very day, I promise!

24

DO YOU WANT TO PROSPER?

3 John 2 (NKJV)
"Beloved, I pray that you may prosper in all things and be in health, just as your soul prospers."

Did you know the Lord desires to prosper you more than you desire to prosper?! No joke!

In fact, the FIRST THING God did after creating humans . . . "Then God blessed them." (Genesis 1:28 NLT) **THE VERY FIRST THING!!!**

Yes, some folks have abused the word "prosperity." But isn't that what satan does EVERY time? As God reveals Truth, hell tries to misconstrue it so we will abandon it altogether.

The Hebrew word for "prospering" means "to push forward" or make progress. (You find "Prospering" SIXTY-THREE TIMES in the Old Testament alone!)

God Himself Longs "To Push Us Forward" In Every Area Of Our Living . . . Our Marriages, Our Children And Grandchildren, Our Finances, Our Health . . . Every Sphere Of Our Existence! But Y'all, It Doesn't Just Fall In Our Laps!

Read our verse again. God prospers us in all things . . . AS OUR SOUL PROSPERS!

In other words, God loves us too much to bless us beyond our ability to manage it. As we live more dependent upon Him, inseparably bonded, He equips and empowers us to handle all He desires to put in our hands.

As we live totally tethered to Jesus, moment by moment, His Presence abides in us. From this posture, we desire nothing more than to obey Him. (Our obedience is the truest indication that our hearts truly belong to Him!)

But how do we obey? It can be so hard, can't it?

You're right, it's hard to muster up sheer willpower to accomplish such a feat! (Been there. Done that!)

But if we truly believe a life of obedience releases the hand of God to "push us forward" (prosperity!), we won't TRY to obey Him; we will WANT to! The more we WANT to, the more our love for the Giver intensifies! This cyclical progression becomes the most beautiful bounty of blessing we've ever known!

God's ways have been put to every test and proven tried and true. If we walk in the ways He established long before we got here, we will eat "the good of the land." (Isaiah 1:19)

Another way of saying it . . . ever-increasing Faith in Jesus brings obedience. Obedience ushers in the Presence of the Lord. And God's manifest Presence in our living brings prosperity in ways we cannot receive through any other means! THIS is the plan of God for our living!

Friend, try as you may, you cannot exaggerate the goodness of God moving in your direction at this very moment! From the very beginning (before you were YOU!) God's heart pulsated with passionate desire to bless you. But He's got to have ALL of you, every crevice of you, to do it!

Without Him, we cannot handle the bounty of the blessing! We just can't!

But with Him at the very center of our living, we both receive the blessing and extend the blessing beyond ourselves, continuously, for the Glory of His Great Name!

God never prospers us for the sake of hoarding blessings. My husband often says, "What we keep weeps. What we give lives."

Let us live generous lives, walking in the ways of the Lord, clinging so tightly to His every Word that we dwell in His Blessing without measure!

What Difference Will This WORD Make In Me?
Feed your faith today with God's Word over your life. Set your heart to obey Him. From this posture, His Presence envelops you. As your soul prospers, watch God prosper other areas of your living in a way that you'll KNOW it was HIM! ALL HIM!

25

COVERING THE FAULT LINES

1 Corinthians 13:7 (AMP)
"Love bears all things."

As long as we live and breathe, conflict, even with those we love, is inescapable. We misinterpret each other's words, motives, or actions, OR we hear them loud and clear! We simply view situations from two VERY different perspectives. It happens.

But amid these inevitabilities, how should the mature one in God respond? We must make amends where possible, so the enemy cannot divide us relationally. More importantly, we must protect ourselves from the rift within that shatters the sanctity of our soul!

God is schooling me on the difference between *forgiveness* and *forbearance.* The mature heart must discern the distinction, then toss the score card!

Forgiveness is when we see the fault lines, and we shore them up by either asking forgiveness or extending it. This grace heals us and moves us forward. Lingering unforgiveness inevitably destroys us from the inside out, NO MATTER who's right! (Get that!)

But what do we do when the pain is screaming, and the person at fault is oblivious or just downright obstinate? If we're not careful, the wound will bleed into every thought until it consumes us. Before long, this colors our words and actions too. That's where forbearance comes in.

"Love bears all things." We "forbear" or "endure" with one another. We cover the unfixed relationship with an endurance only God can give. (Stay with me!)

"Love covers a multitude of sins." (1 Peter 4:8) That doesn't mean we become a doormat or gloss over the wrongs done. Such a view distorts grace instead of walking in its power.

The grace God gives to forbear or endure doesn't ignore or deny the mistreatment It simply sets us in a place in God where we can say "love never fails" ...in me! No matter the chasms between this person and me now, God's love in me covers the gaps just as He has covered my own shortcomings with Himself.

I know, I know. You're probably thinking that the disagreement stretches too far. Trying to forgive or forbear feels contrived. This rift is NOT resolved. I hear you! But stop waiting on the other party to act. It's not even about them any longer. It's about YOU and the sanctity of your own soul.

God covered the gaping hole between you and Him. Now He empowers *you* to cover the broken places in this situation. His love at work in you fastens the fault lines together because His love never fails . . . in you!

"But what about the wrong inflicted? What about the mistreatment leveled against me?"

Remember, I'm talking to mature ones! Get your eyes off that person and become fixed on God's unfailing love toward you.

You're Not Trying To Prove Your Point.
You Are Proving God's Love
Is Alive And Well IN YOU!
Rushing Waters Cannot Squelch
That Kind Of Love
And Floods Cannot Drown It.

God is not asking you to become chums again. He is requiring of you a love that takes the high road and fills the chasm. It's the only way to experience freedom from this situation. Otherwise, this offense becomes a stronghold that strangles the life blood out of you!

Ditch the offense, friend. Stop letting it preoccupy your thoughts. Choose to love anyway! Consider God's extravagant love toward you that poured over your broken pieces when He owed you NOTHING! From that place, you can walk through the rubble on your way to climbing higher!

"Love knows no limit to its endurance, no end to its trust, no fading of its hope; it can outlast anything. It is, in fact, the one thing that still stands when all else has fallen." (1 Corinthians 13:7-8a PHILLIPS)

What Difference Will This WORD Make In Me?

Let's do something audacious, mature one. This person that hurt you? Let's call his or her name to the Lord today. Let's pray God's blessing upon their lives in such a way that they cannot help but see HIM and sense His love that empowered you to cover the fault lines.

26

ARISE

Isaiah 60:1-3 (NASB)
"Arise, shine; for YOUR light has come,
And the Glory of the Lord has risen upon YOU.
For behold, darkness will cover the earth
And deep darkness the peoples;
BUT THE LORD WILL RISE UPON YOU!
AND HIS GLORY WILL APPEAR UPON YOU!"

WHEW! Friend, I don't think I need to convince you that darkness feels darker these days. Those who distain the one true God are becoming quite brazen. The spirit of Jezebel (that is, the motive of manipulation, vile and vicious) is running rampant and causing most folks to react with paralyzing fear about the future.

God used His prophet, Isaiah, to speak to a time reminiscent to ours. He used A PROPHET...you know, those people who are getting mocked into oblivion right now because every true prophet looks like an idiot *until they don't.* (ANYWHO...back to Isaiah....)

Isaiah spoke to God's People standing upon the ruins of the life they had previously known. The work to rebuild their lives and communities proved much more daunting than they had imagined. Challenges multiplied by the hour. Circumstances grew more dire by the day. These difficulties had dragged on entirely too long! (Does that not sound eerily like our world since the drastic changes in 2020?)

Despite everything God's Prophets had spoken, Jerusalem still resembled a mere shadow of the great city their parents and grandparents remembered. People began doubting whether God had really spoken or was even there. Was He truly able? Did He remotely care?

But there was that Remnant of folks who knew...

GOD IS EVERYTHING He Says He Is, And HE DOES EVERYTHING He Says He Does!

That small group of Great Faith-ers determined to convince the naysayers that God COULD restore that people and that place to greatness again. They believed that indeed HE WOULD if they pursued His Glory above everything else! AND HE DID!!!

Those same words God spoke to Isaiah for that time speaks resoundingly to this time in history. God is essentially saying, "ARISE from your depression concerning the circumstances that have tried to keep you down. Stop lying there in despair. GET UP! As you begin to ARISE, God's Glory will appear through you; and when you stand with the visible brilliance of God's Glory upon you, you will have everything you need to take down the principalities and powers that thought they took you down!" (That's the Lanier Translation!)

Friends, God is birthing a thing in us right now that is so necessary for all that is coming. When the world gets darker, the Remnant (that's us!) must become more brilliant with His Glory. In that place, the whole earth will see and know His Magnificence!

It's on US, believers in Jesus! This is OUR responsibility AND our privilege! We are this world's only HOPE! Let us ARISE!

What Difference Will This WORD Make In Me?

As you stand in dark places today, declare Isaiah 60. Put a sticky note on your computer. ARISE! SHINE! Be Light in THAT place so that His Glory becomes visible through YOU! Jesus glistening through YOU . . . it is their only Hope!

27

WHEN SUFFERING COMES KNOCKING AT YOUR DOOR

1 Peter 2:21-25 (MSG)
*"This is the kind of life you've been invited into,
the kind of life Christ lived.
He suffered everything that came His way
so you would know that it could be done,
and also know how to do it, step-by-step.
He never did one thing wrong,
Not once said anything amiss.
They called Him every name in the book and
He said nothing back. He suffered in silence,
content to let God set things right.
He used His servant body to carry our sins
to the Cross so we could be rid of sin,
free to live the right way.
HIS WOUNDS BECAME YOUR HEALING!
You were lost sheep with no idea*

who you were or where you were going.
Now you're named and kept for good
by the Shepherd of your souls."

Who doesn't run for the hills when suffering barrels in our direction? I've been to no doctor about this condition, but I feel confident that I am allergic to pain.

Peter penned these words as authorities bore down hard on believers in Jesus. Nero, a savage dictator, sought to completely obliterate the Church that just kept multiplying even under extreme persecution. Many who stood for Christ paid with their very lives. (Martyrs for Jesus, then and now, inspire me so deeply!)

Peter wrote to encourage families facing hardships they'd never known. His words speak to us right where we live too! (Are you facing hardship like you've never known?!)

Some folks may say that living for Jesus exempts us from suffering. They may mean well, but they are wrong!

Living for Jesus absolutely cocoons us from some situations. God hedges us, becoming our wrap-around shield. As we abide in Him and His Word abides in us, we walk with an unfair advantage. My whole life testifies of this Truth!

Nevertheless, until we see Jesus face-to-face, we live in a world that perpetuates trouble.

Some Of What We Face Is Self-inflicted. Other Times, Our Pain Has Nothing To Do With Our Decisions. In Fact, At Times We Suffer Precisely *BECAUSE* We Are Doing the Right Thing!

If you're still not having any of this "suffering" chat, then remember the anguish Jesus endured when *"He never did one thing wrong, Not once said anything amiss. They called Him every name in the book and He said nothing back. He suffered in silence, content to let God set things right."* (2:21)...AND GOD DID SET THINGS RIGHT!

Peter reminds us that Jesus "is our example and we follow in His steps!" (2:21)

"Example" here refers to a person learning to write. The student copies each letter carefully until he can replicate the example effortlessly.

THIS is the life Christ called us to live! Even amid turbulence that threatens to capsize our boat, we refuse to rehearse the unfairness of the storm. We refuse to nurture self-pity about it. Instead, we choose to keep charging toward the shoreline where victory awaits.

Suffering does not diminish us; it advances us toward the place of triumph!

Listen friend, "JESUS' WOUNDS [HIS SUFFERING] BECAME YOUR HEALING!" (1:24)

God will redeem anything (ANYTHING!) offered back to Him. Can we have the audacity to believe that what we endure right now can be, WILL BE, used to benefit His Great Name AND our good?!

Can we dare to believe this seemingly hopeless situation can actually prove beneficial beyond what we can see in this moment?

As I lay my whole life on the altar, I invite God to redeem even THIS impossible season!

So let us keep meticulously following Christ's example, letter by letter, until we replicate His steadfastness even through the hardest moments of life.

As we DAILY lay ourselves on the altar of surrender, let us believe that God can resurrect even this hard thing and set things right! He can! And I declare by God HE WILL!

What Difference Does This WORD Make In Me?
Name the hard thing that brings tremendous pain to your living in this season. Choose this day to forfeit all complaining about its unfairness. Follow Jesus' example to the letter believing as we glorify God even in THIS situation, He will come and sets things right!

28

IT WILL BE WORTH IT ALL

1 Corinthians 16:13 (tPt)
*"Remember to stay alert and hold firmly
to all that you believe.
Be mighty and full of courage."*

Have you ever been knocked off your high horse? I've been too big for my britches more than a time or two. While I still don't have a clue what my britches have to do with anything, I know enough about the New Testament to know that a man on a mission got knocked off his high horse as he arrogantly galloped toward Jesus Lovers to destroy them.

Remember that guy Saul, who considered it his personal responsibility to terrorize Christians until he ridded the world of every last one of them? Saul stood

133

with the mob that stoned the first Christian martyr, Stephen, to death. Now, rampaged against anyone who dared proclaim the Resurrected LORD.

It's noteworthy to mention that when that moment came for God to deal with this enemy of His Church, He didn't even mention the Church. (It's the Truth. Look it up!)

Once Saul toppled off his high horse, the LORD confronted this tyrant, "Saul, Saul, why are you persecuting ME?" (Acts 26:14 NLT)

In short, Jesus took the mistreatment of His People deeply personally. He viewed every attack as if the perpetrator had targeted Christ Himself! Jesus was saying, "When you mess with one of Mine, you're messing with ME!"

Today is also an increasingly difficult time to call Jesus, "LORD". As we watch godless agendas materialize, we discern the heavy hand targeting the Church. We've never seen a more unholy, unbiblical itinerary emerge in this nation's history. The heat is on, and those refusing to play along with the charade will pay a high price. This Faith-filled life is certainly not for the faint of heart. It's why so many Church attendees lost their way in the shutdown and still haven't found their footing.

I've been in the Church my whole life. I'll be the first to admit that God's People carry shortcomings. (Have you ever met even one human who didn't??) But I also know that God's true Remnant is the only HOPE for planet earth! While world systems arrogantly assume we need them, it is they who need us. (We don't brag on ourselves; we're bragging on our LORD!)

True Christians Are Not Better THAN Anyone Else But We ARE Unequivocally Better FOR Everyone Else!

God's Remnant knows we are the last firewall against hell's diabolical plans in the earth, and hell knows it too!

As I pen these thoughts, I can't help but consider our brothers and sisters in Afghanistan. Afghanistan's underground Church is the second fastest-growing church in the world, only behind Iran's. Those Believers risk *all* for their faith!

As the Taliban conquered Afghanistan in 2021, terrorists invaded believers' homes, brutalized them mercilessly, then shot them dead for sport.

The courage of these Christ-followers floods my face with tears and infuses my soul with such resolve. Even dying, they refused to recant this most Holy Faith. They were THAT certain that God is true to everything He's promised and that He awaits their arrival.

The enemy is coming for what he's most afraid of...THE CHURCH, the ones who stand sure in battle with THE NAME on our side.

But for the True Bride of Christ, we've never been more certain that we stand on solid ground that cannot be shaken amid the shaking!

Take heart, People of the Living God. When Jehovah's enemies come against His Church, He takes it very personally. When God steps in to deal with it (and He will!), the arrogant ones will fall off their high horse! Mark my word. Better yet, mark His Word. It never fails!

Meanwhile, brothers and sisters, stay humble and sure, focused and full of hope. I promise you with every ounce of my being...it will be worth it all!

What Difference Will This WORD Make In Me?
Consider ways this very day to get your brave on for the One who bravely stood up for you! Speak up! Be counted among those willing to pay the price!

29

RUNNING WITH THE HORSES

Jeremiah 12:5 (ERV)
*"If running in a race against men makes you tired,
how will you race against horses?
If you trip and fall in a safe place,
what will you do in a dangerous place?"*

Have you ever felt so worn down that your giddy-up gets good and gone? I'm talking about those moments when you give in because you're "plumb give out!"

You know exactly what I'm talking about. We all face those seasons when life feels unfair. We offer God all we've got; STILL, we hit a wall. It seems evildoers flourish while God's faithful ones feel the heat for living right. Before long, self-pity seeps in and digs a ditch of despair within us.

The Prophet Jeremiah found himself in this pitiful place. God called Jeremiah to sound the alarm to church folks acting a fool. But no matter how relentlessly Jeremiah raised his voice, nothing changed. Hearts got harder. Ears got deafer. His obedience felt futile!

We humans long to live meaningful lives. We need to know our contribution to this world matters. When it appears pointless, we struggle to keep going.

In one of these despairing times, Jeremiah considered throwing in the towel. He cried out to the Lord, craving comfort. But God knew solace was the last thing His faithful one needed.

As Jeremiah questioned Yahweh's purpose in this seeming nonsense, God doubled down. He spoke to the warrior hiding inside Jeremiah. (He speaks to the warrior living inside YOU too!)

God responded, *"If running in a race against men makes you tired, how will you race against horses? If you trip and fall in a safe place, what will you do in a dangerous place?"*

Essentially, He asks, "Are you seriously ready to quit at the first wave of opposition? If you can't manage THIS, how will you handle the greater things I have assigned for your living? Surely, you didn't think this was going to be easy. Living a significant life never is! Get your brave on, mighty one! You are not average. Stop acting average!" (Whew, I felt that!)

This is it:

Crowds Dodge Pain To Protect Themselves. Consequently, They Never Overcome! When They Reach The End Of Their Days, Their Risk-Free Living Leaves No Mark. Their Benign Existence Makes No Difference.

When we belong to God, we don't seek exemption from hard things. We actually enlist for challenging times, knowing He made us to overcome! God provides the supernatural capacity to walk through dangerous places with courage that conquers the very thing seeking to conquer us.

Scripture doesn't record Jeremiah's verbal response to God's question. But as we study this prophet's heroic life, we realize that the rest of his days declared, *"I'll run with the horses!"*

Listen friend, if mere disappointment can stop us, we'll stop! Don't choose less because less is easy. Don't quit now because significance is hard. We've got to expect hard things, because we were made to run against the current of the crowds. We were created to leave a lasting mark that matters long after we're gone.

It's time for you to believe in you like God believes in you! Get back on your feet. Stand in confidence and great courage. If God called you to this, *you can do it!* In fact, as you lean into Him with all you've got, He'll give you HIS strength and stamina. You were made to run with the horses…AND WIN!

What Difference Will This WORD Make In Me?
Stop rehearsing all the reasons this season of life feels unfair. Stop allowing disappointment to lay so heavy on you that you want to quit. Make up your mind this day that you WILL live a significant life of faith. You WILL leave a mark that lasts beyond you, for God's Glory and for the good of your generations! Let's get to it!

140

30

I'M STICKING WITH IT!

Jeremiah 1:11-12 (MSG)
"God's Message came to me:
"What do you see, Jeremiah?"
I said, "A walking stick—that's all."
And God said, "Good eyes! I'm sticking with you.
I'll make every word I give you come true."

Have you ever stood in winter's chill and struggled to believe that spring would know its way back to you?

When you stand amid life's stinging temps, surveying those things that failed to survive the severity of the season, that same lifelessness can seep thick into your own soul, can't it? Hope for the turnaround you need seems utterly impossible.

Friend, you've got to get this! The "walking stick" God placed before the prophet Jeremiah in that season was actually a branch from an almond tree. That may seem completely random but hear me...God does NOTHING by chance! (Stay with me!)

An almond tree is one of the few trees that bloom in the winter. Even before leaves appear, blossoms sprout. It's the darndest thing! Right in the middle of winter's chill, blooms dare to promise that spring is surely on its way!

The bitter cold strives to snuff out those hints of hope; but despite its power to kill other living things, frost fails here. The barren reality of winter cannot halt this tree from doing what God created it to do!

When the Lord downloaded The Power of His Promise to a listening soul that day, He chose THIS tree as a reminder to you THIS day that no matter what this moment looks like, a new season is rushing toward you now! God WILL finish what He promised!

Folks, God Has Spoken His Word
Over Your Living As Sure and Steady
As Your Next Breath.
In Fact, Hell Is Surer of God's Word
Over Your Life Than You Are!

It's why, when you find yourself in frosty times, the enemy of your soul seeks to confuse and distort what you know to be true.

But you and I must remember that God is good for His Promise! If He says so, it IS so! He sticks to it and does the heavy lifting. He simply asks us to stick with Him and believe Him no matter what we see in the barren place.

As you stand smackdab in the middle of things that feel dead and done, the Lord comes to whisper hope into your heart today:

I have not forgotten or forsaken My Word over your life. I have not walked away from all I Promised! I'm sticking to My Word over you like a shepherd sticks with his sheep.

Not even one word will wander away. Not one word will be lost! I'm sure of it! As long as you stick close and stay close even when you don't understand, My Word will be accomplished in you, period! A new season is moving toward you now! Stick with Me and watch Me do it!

What Difference Will This WORD Make In Me?
You likely feel like Jeremiah, so incapable and inadequate to do anything of real significance. It's hard to believe that what God is saying over your life can actually happen through YOU as you see everything opposite surrounding you.

As you read these two verses over your life today, look for the stick God has placed before you. Declare by Faith throughout this day... "God's Word will bloom even as I stand in barren times. IT WILL!"

31

FULLY CONVINCED!

Romans 4:21 (NET)
*"He was fully convinced that
what God promised He was also able to do."*

Do you have people in your life who seem to see the best in every situation? If you don't, you need them!

My Daddy is one of the most optimistic people I know. Every time I call him, I sense the smile in his voice. Daddy answers, "Every day is a good day!" No matter what has tried his soul, whether serious sickness or even the death of his precious wife, Daddy somehow recognizes things could be worse. For real!

This high-octane optimism drives the pessimist nuts! It even rubs the realist the wrong way at times. But when you're fighting your way out of a difficult situation, you need someone who believes it can get better despite what you see.

Some folks would deem Abraham, the father of our faith, an optimist. What else could account for his ability to believe for the best when not even a smidgen of that reality had come into view?

God promised a decrepit old man he would become a father to multitudes, when he and his barren wife (INFERTILE!) had never been able to conceive even one child in their youth!

Think about it. God promised them that they would soon be changing baby diapers in a season when they actually wore diapers. (Depends® sounds kinder, doesn't it?)

Abraham's wife, Sarah, found it impossible to conceive a child long before menopause At age 90 with a hundred-year-old husband, the thought was laughable! In fact, that's precisely what Sarah did when she caught wind of this nonsense. She laughed! (Cackled, really.)

Yet despite endless waiting, despite obstacles that heightened the impossibility of this absurdity... Abraham believed!

The Scriptures say, "AGAINST ALL ODDS, when it looked hopeless, Abraham believed the Promise and expected God to fulfill it. He took God at His Word. He never stopped believing God's Promise, for he was made strong in his Faith. And because he was mighty in Faith and convinced that God had all the Power needed to fulfill His Promises, Abraham glorified God and became the father of many nations." (Romans 4:18; 20-21 tPt)

Folks, steadfast belief in spite of every impossibility is so much more than optimism; it's unadulterated Faith!

Even Optimism Has An Expiration Date.
The Most Positive-Thinking Person
Will Hit A Limit And Falter.
But When We Feed Our Faith
In The God Who Cannot Lie,
We Can Keep Believing
No Matter How Many Times
We Get Knocked Down!

Are you getting this?! There was zero reason to believe God could do this through them. None! Yet Abraham was "...FULLY CONVINCED that what God had promised, He was also able to do!" (4:21 NET)

This is the best definition of Faith out there! Did God say it? Can God pull off what He said? Faith remains FULLY CONVINCED!

Friends and family surrounding Abraham surely reminded him of all the reasons he should move on and forget this pipe dream, probably rehearsed with meticulous detail why this absurdity could never happen. Yet, Abraham chose to rehearse the Promise of God more emphatically than all the skepticism surrounding him.

Friends, we must do this, too! Some people will feel obligated to remind you of all the reasons "it" can never work. Many of them love you deeply. But they can't see what you see. They can't hear what you hear. Their reference point resides in the natural; but your reference point in GOD dwells in the supernatural!

What Difference Will This WORD Make In Me?

What impossibility faces you today? What does God's Word say about it? In spite of what stands in your way, stand on that Word and rehearse it over and again until you are "...FULLY CONVINCED that what God has promised, He is also able to do!"

ACKNOWLEDGEMENTS

Has everything revved up around us or what? Attempting to pen another devotional book amid the craziness is definitely not for wimps. Nevertheless, we've never needed God's Word as our compass more than now. So, I fight for it!

As I typed each devotional, the most amazing team surrounded me! They helped reach the finish line despite all they juggle in their own lives. Let's just make this clear...you wouldn't be reading this book if these gifted girls had not jumped into the deep waters with me.

Shout-out to my excellent editor, Lisa Jones. She not only cleans up my work in this book; she edits a monthly column I write for Forsyth Woman Magazine. I'm telling you; Lisa lives in the trenches with me. She knows what I'm going to say before I say it. That's how many miles we've journeyed together. I could NEVER do this without her! She's a true champion to my heart!

Then there's my childhood friend, Lori Hayes. She comes out from hiding on occasion just for me. I'm always honored. She's been a tried-and-true friend since middle school (told ya it's been a hot minute!). Lori's genius mind formats every page, making it ready for publishing AND for Kindle reading. She can figure out ANYTHING! I love her so!

Another longtime friend, Kim Porter, spent hours tightening each devotional's consistency. She often says, "I'll do anything you need." Everyone says that, don't they? The difference is...Kim really means it! I adore her!

Jodie Brim Photography captured the cover shot with such excellence. Jodie can make ANYBODY look picture ready! She's off-the-charts amazing!

My one-of-a-kind daughter created this cover. She runs circles around me these days managing everything on her plate. STILL, she does it all with excellence. I'm so proud of her! She's my at-all-times Worshipping Jesus girl!

I'm just so grateful for this team's wholehearted devotion to God's Unchanging, Unconquerable Word.

They wanted it in your hands as much as I did! I'm tremendously blessed by their bright light and generous hearts every day of the week!

ALSO BY THIS AUTHOR

SOMETHING IN ALL OF US WANTS TO DO BETTER, BE BETTER. WE JUST FIGHT LIKE THE DICKENS TO GET THERE, DON'T WE? HE FULLY INTENDS FOR US TO ACT UPON ALL HE REVEALS.

AS GOD'S WORD TAKES ROOT AND GETS ACTIVATED IN US, PARCHED AREAS BEGIN TO BLOOM AND DEAD THINGS COME TO LIFE! FOR REAL! HE'S CHANGING YOU AND ME, YOU KNOW?

THE ONLY WAY TO GET TO WHERE WE WANT TO BE IS FORWARD. LET'S HOLD HANDS AND GET THERE TOGETHER!

LISTEN CLOSE, FRIEND. "GOD IS NOT A MAN—HE DOESN'T LIE. [HE DOESN'T] TAKE BACK WHAT HE'S SAID, OR SAY SOMETHING AND NOT FOLLOW THROUGH, OR SPEAK AND NOT ACT ON IT." (NUMBERS 23:19, VOICE) GOD CAN BE TRUSTED WITH YOU AND EVERY SINGLE THING THAT CONCERNS YOU. HE IS NOT MERELY ENOUGH. GOD'S WORD IS MORE THAN YOU'LL EVER NEED!

COME DIVE INTO THESE PAGES WITH ME. LET'S PUT GOD'S WORD TO THE TEST AND WATCH IT TRIUMPH IN YOUR LIFE JUST LIKE IT HAS EVERY OTHER TIME THROUGHOUT THE AGES FOR THOSE WHO BELIEVED GOD'S LIVING WORD MORE THAN THEY BELIEVED ANYTHING ELSE!

AVAILABLE ON AMAZON

Made in the USA
Columbia, SC
24 November 2023

26654388R00095